Let that Shit Go!

A SWEARY AND NOT-SO-SWEARY COLORING BOOK FOR ADULTS

By
Tina Indalecio

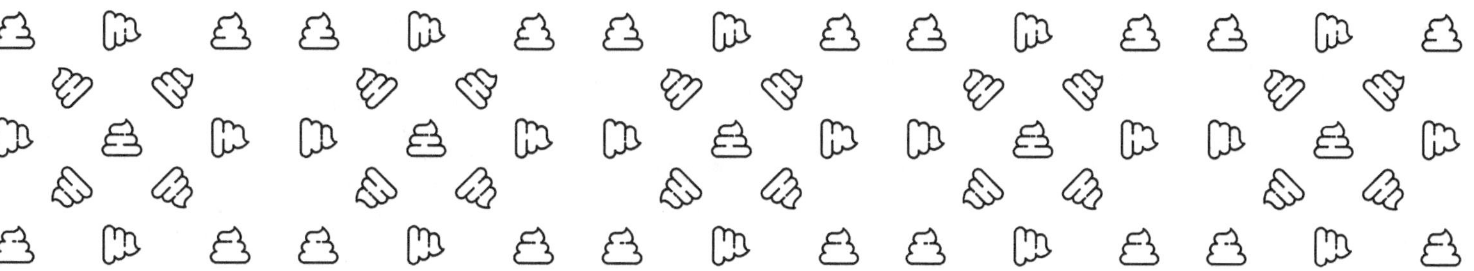

ISBN: 979-8-9898457-0-5

This coloring book is dedicated to
all the people who have had enough of
other people's shit!

May you find peace, happiness, and joy as you
color your way to letting go, and no longer giving a shit!

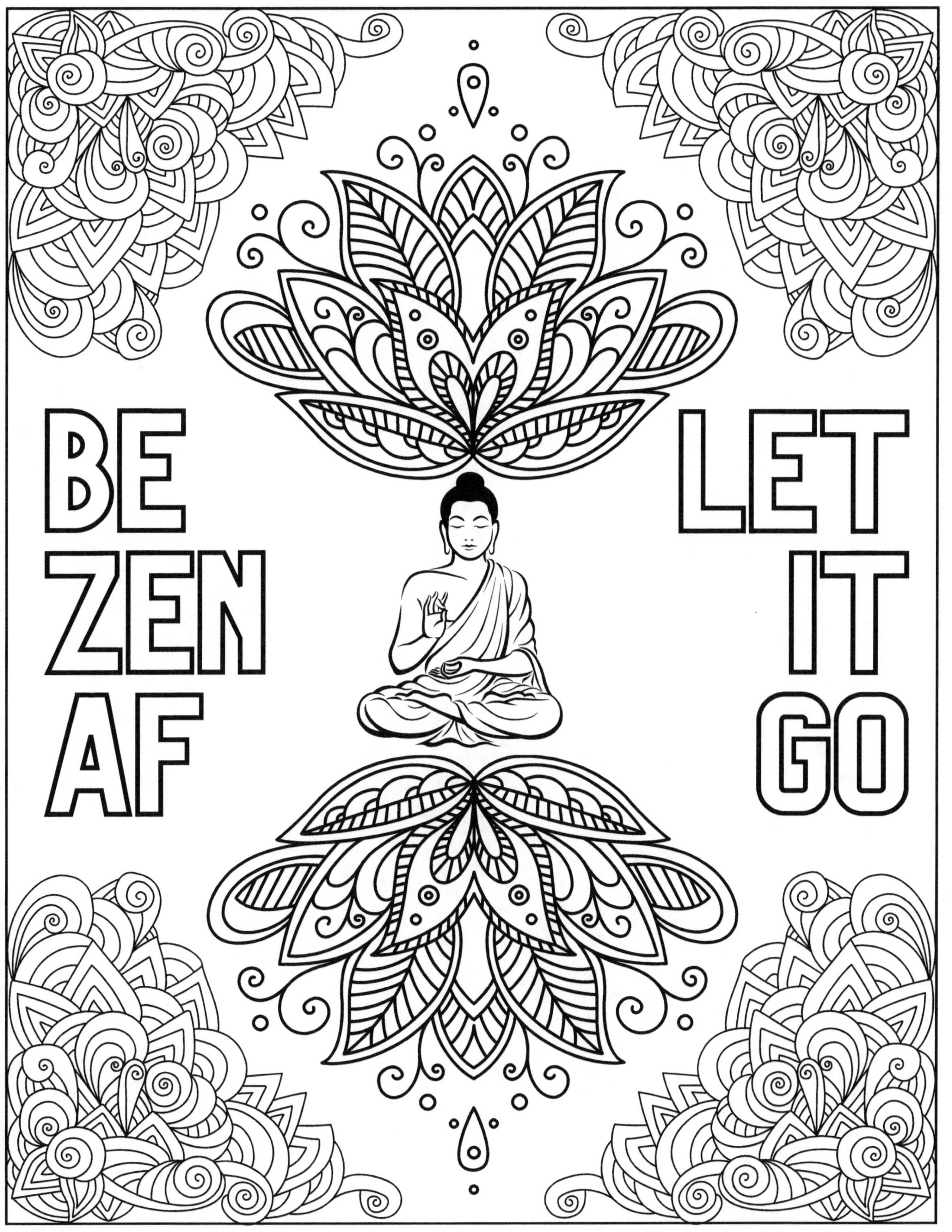
BE
ZEN
AF
LET
IT
GO

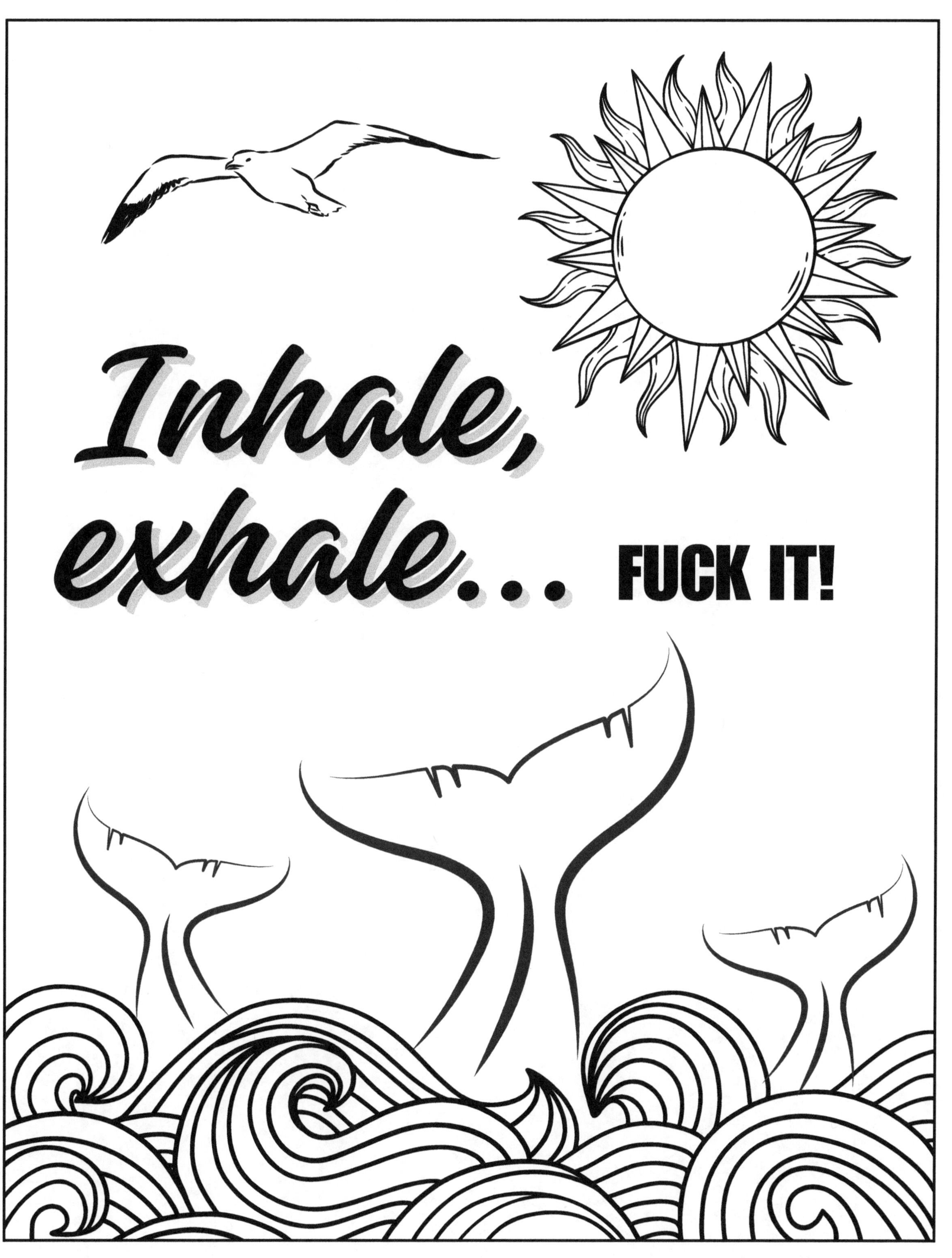
Inhale,
exhale...
FUCK IT!

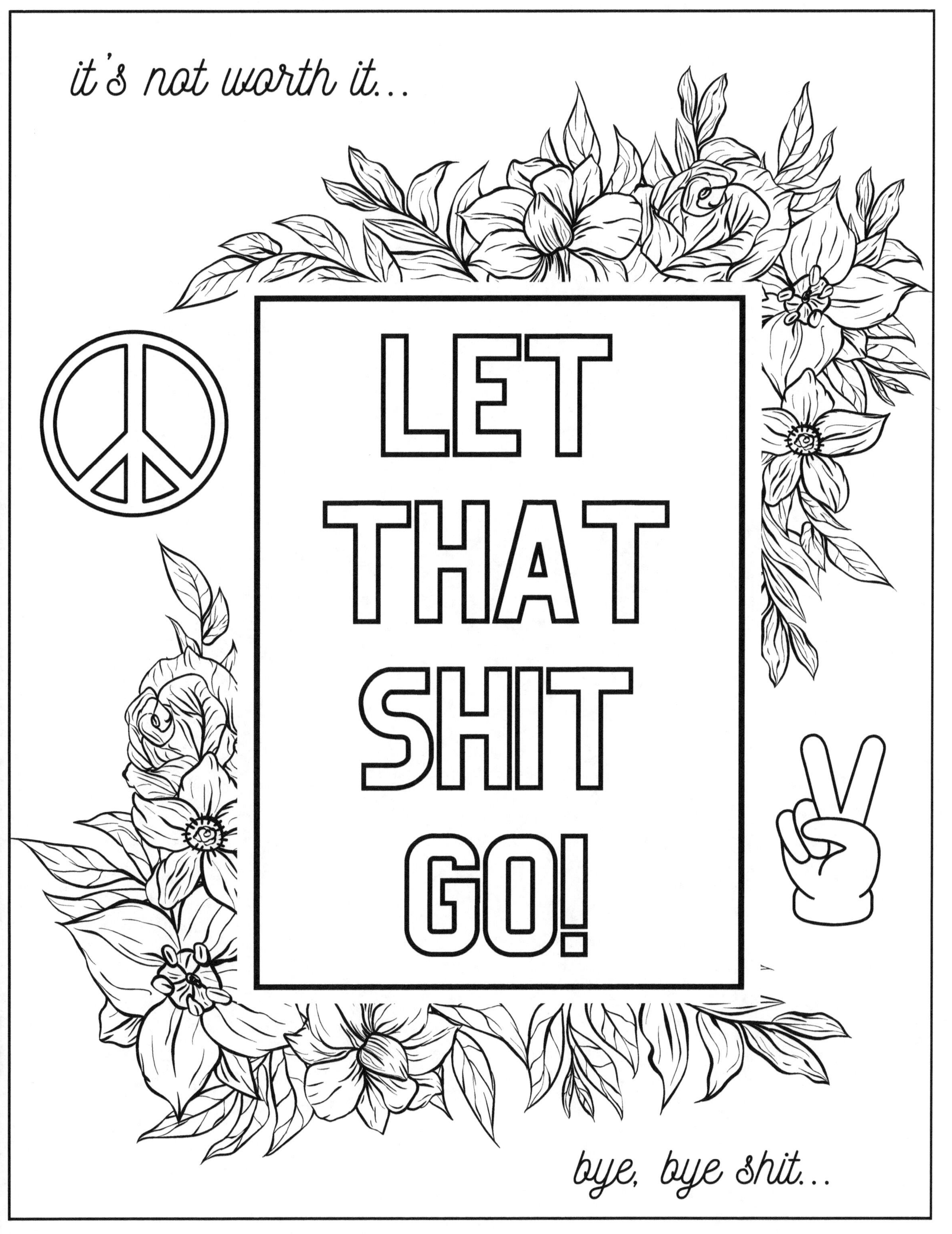
it's not worth it...
LET
THAT
SHIT
GO!
bye, bye shit...

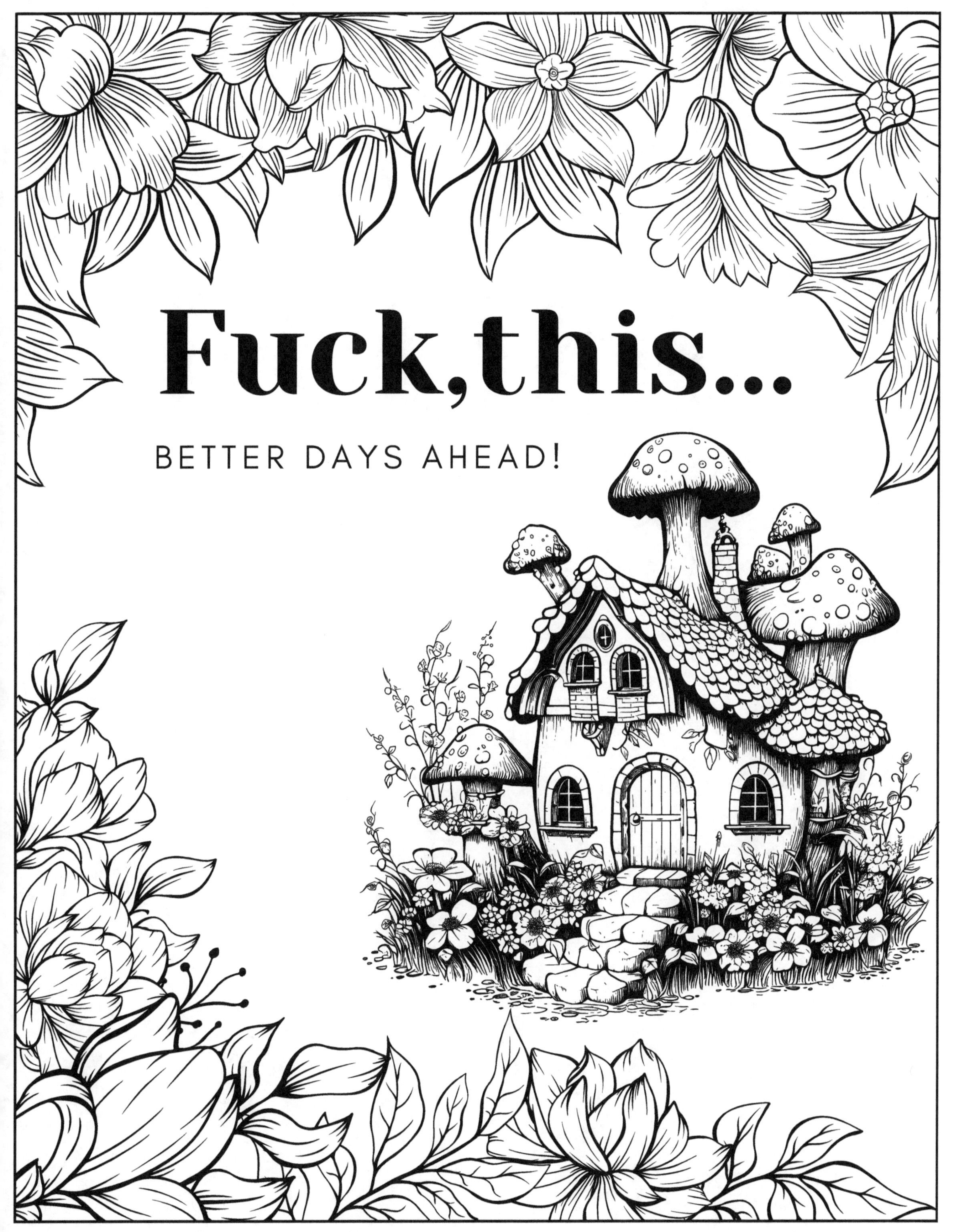
Fuck, this...
BETTER DAYS AHEAD!

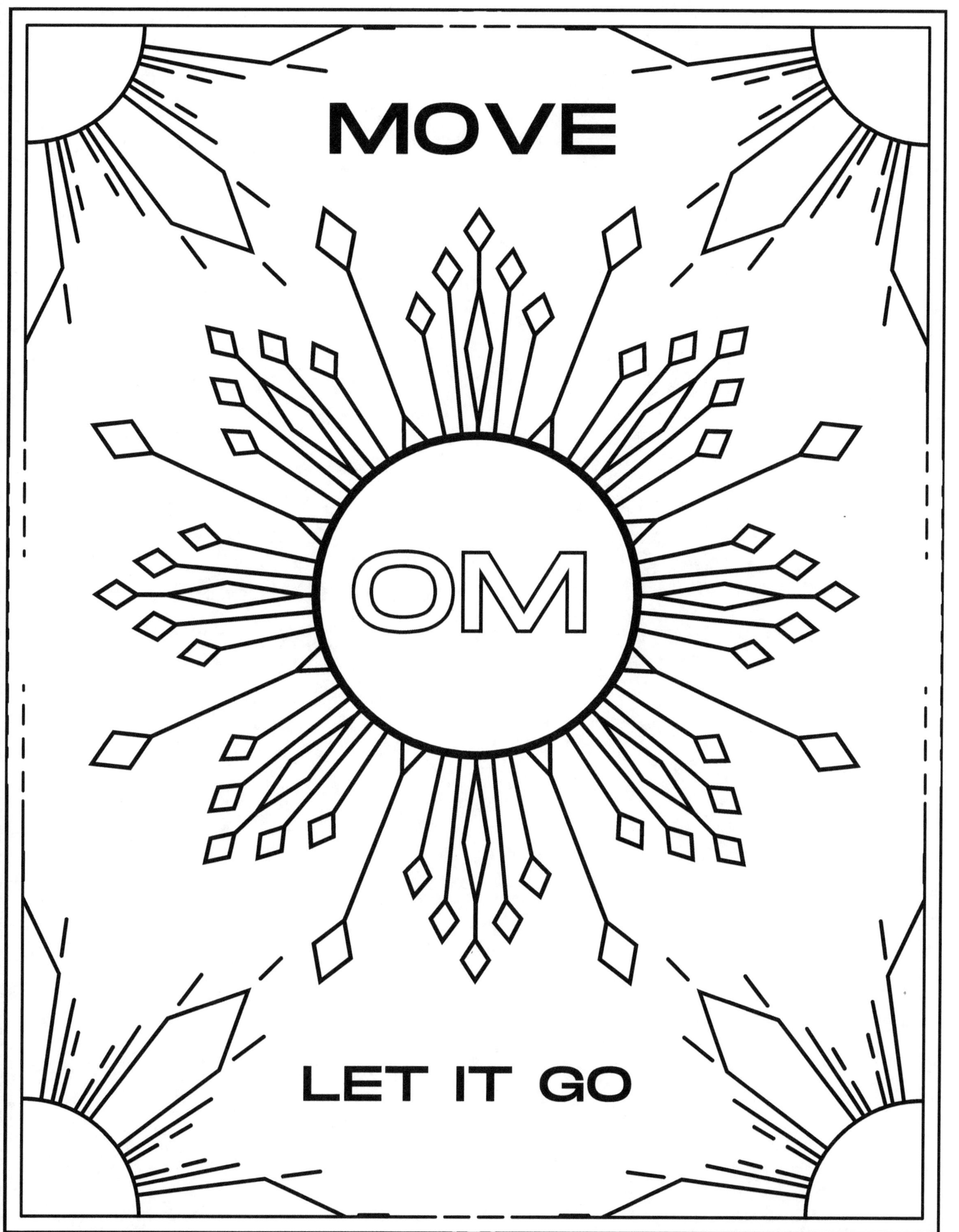
MOVE
OM
LET IT GO

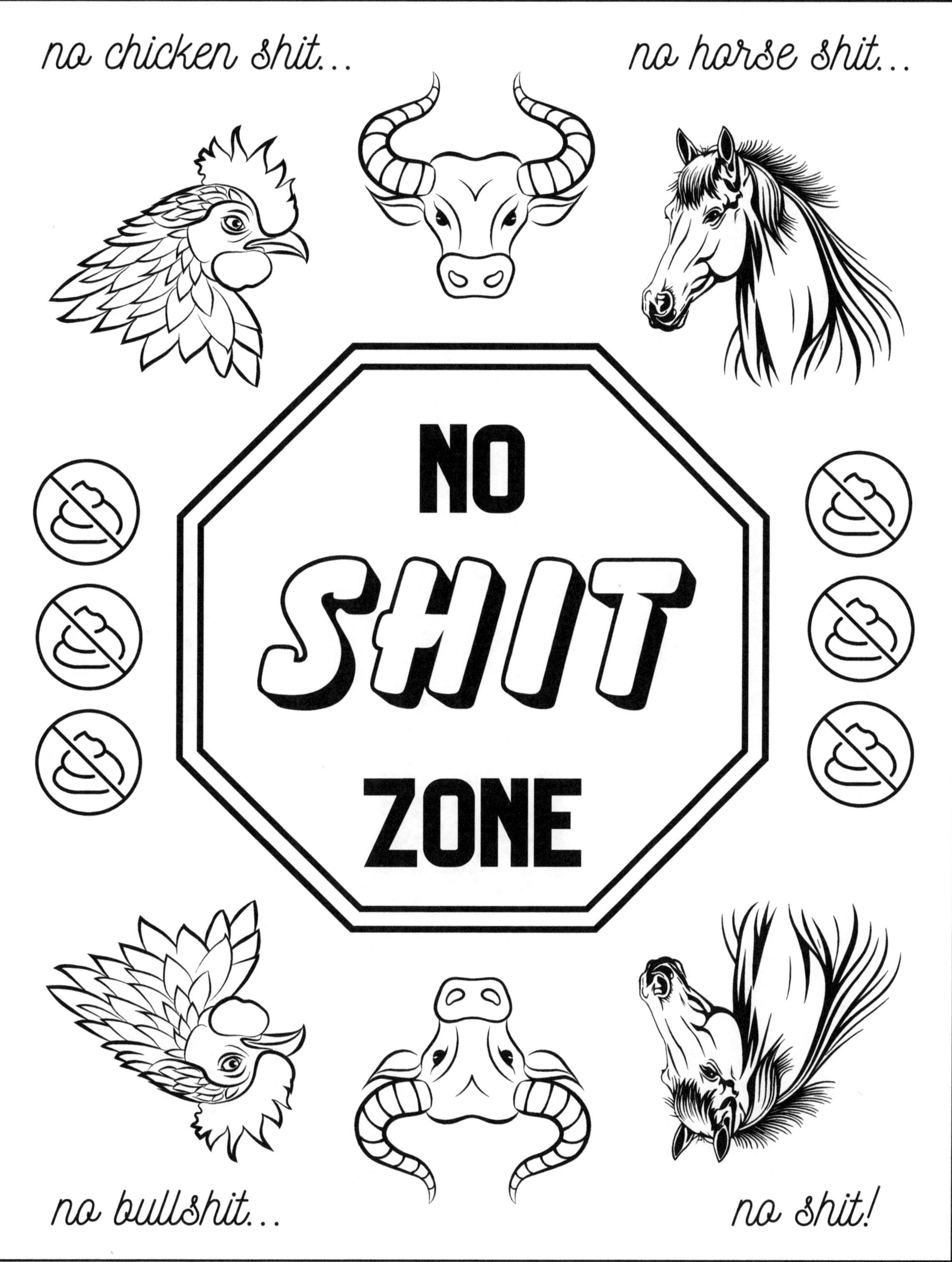
no chicken shit...
no horse shit...
NO
SHIT
ZONE
no bullshit...
no shit!

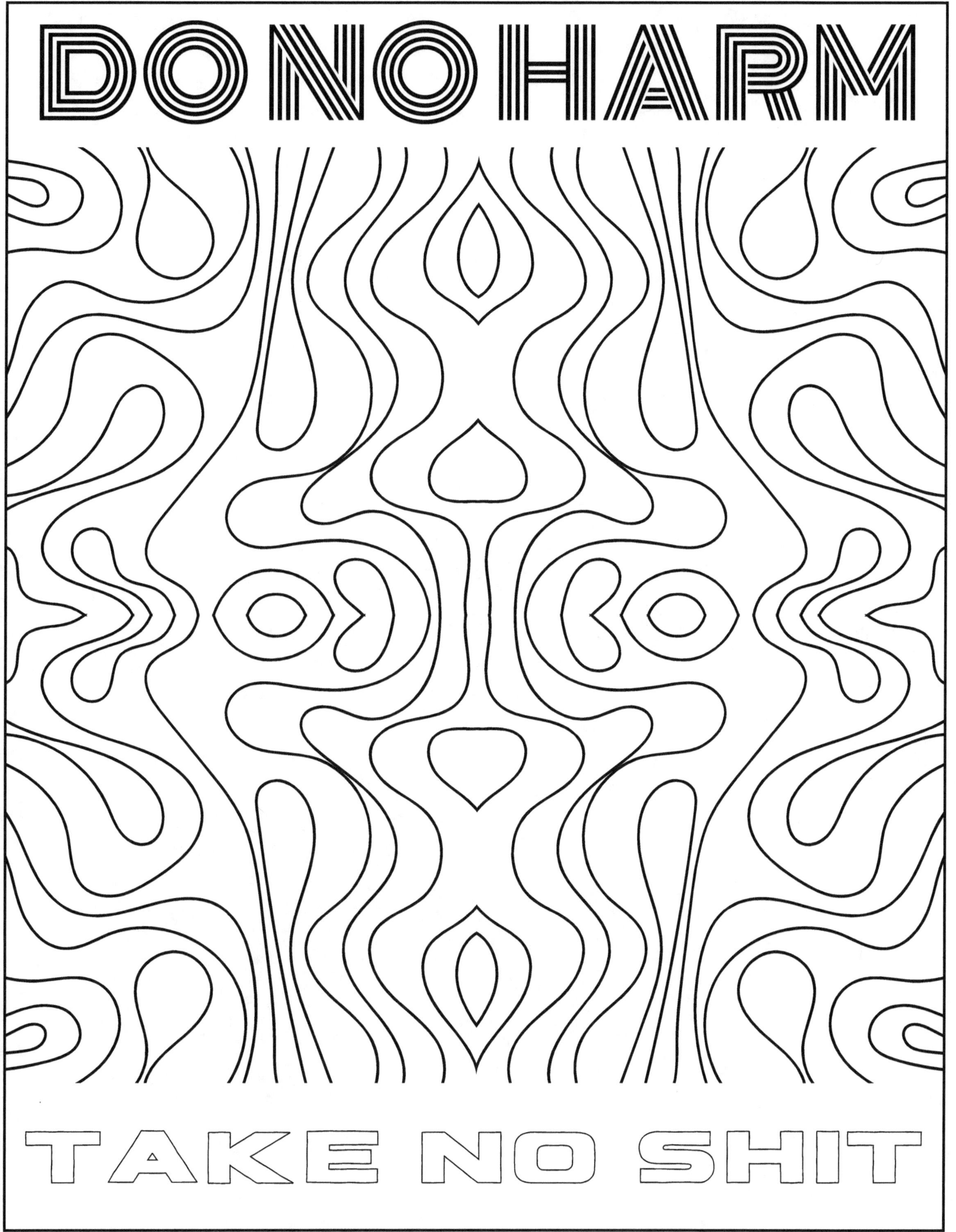
DO NO HARM
TAKE NO SHIT

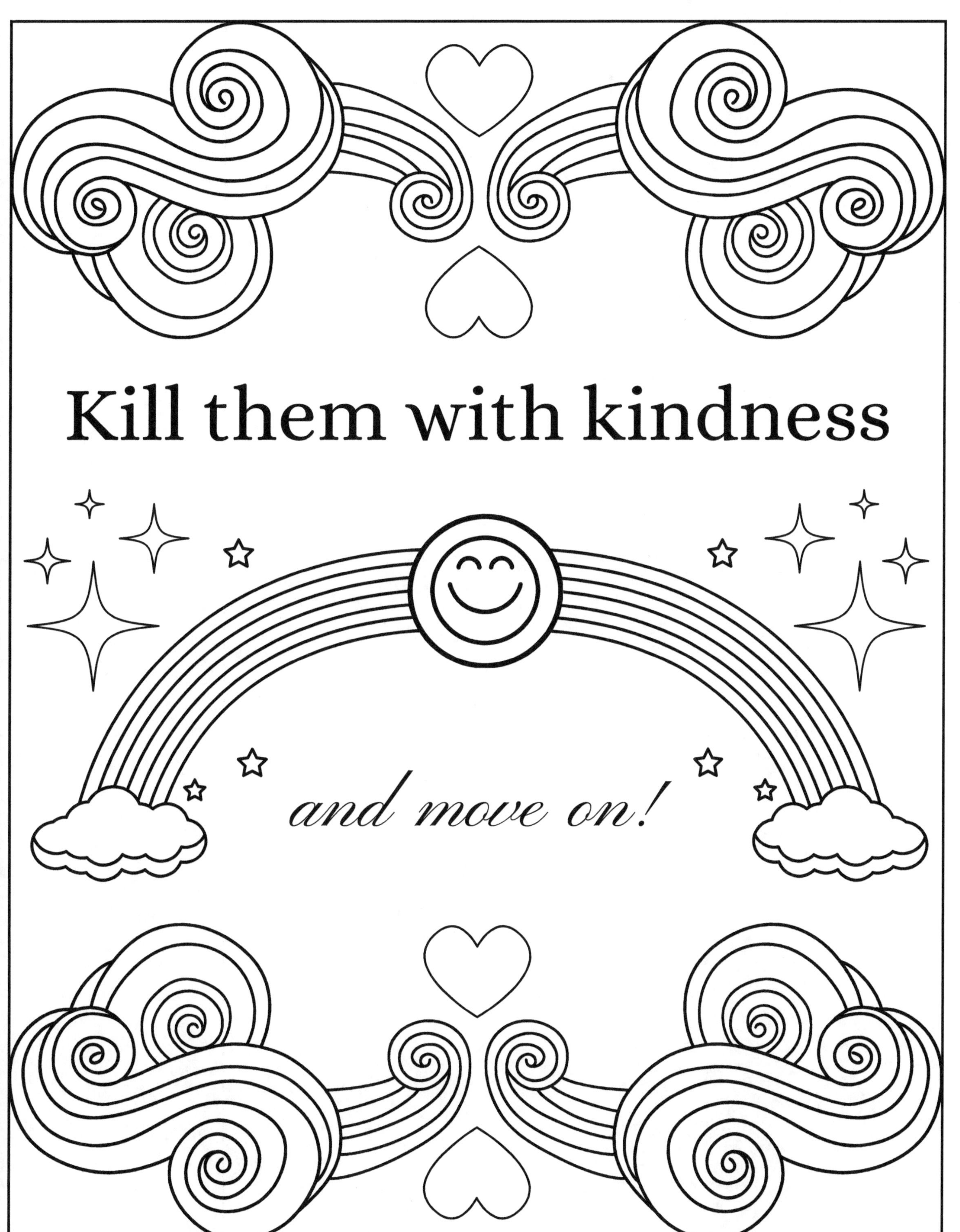
Kill them with kindness
and move on!

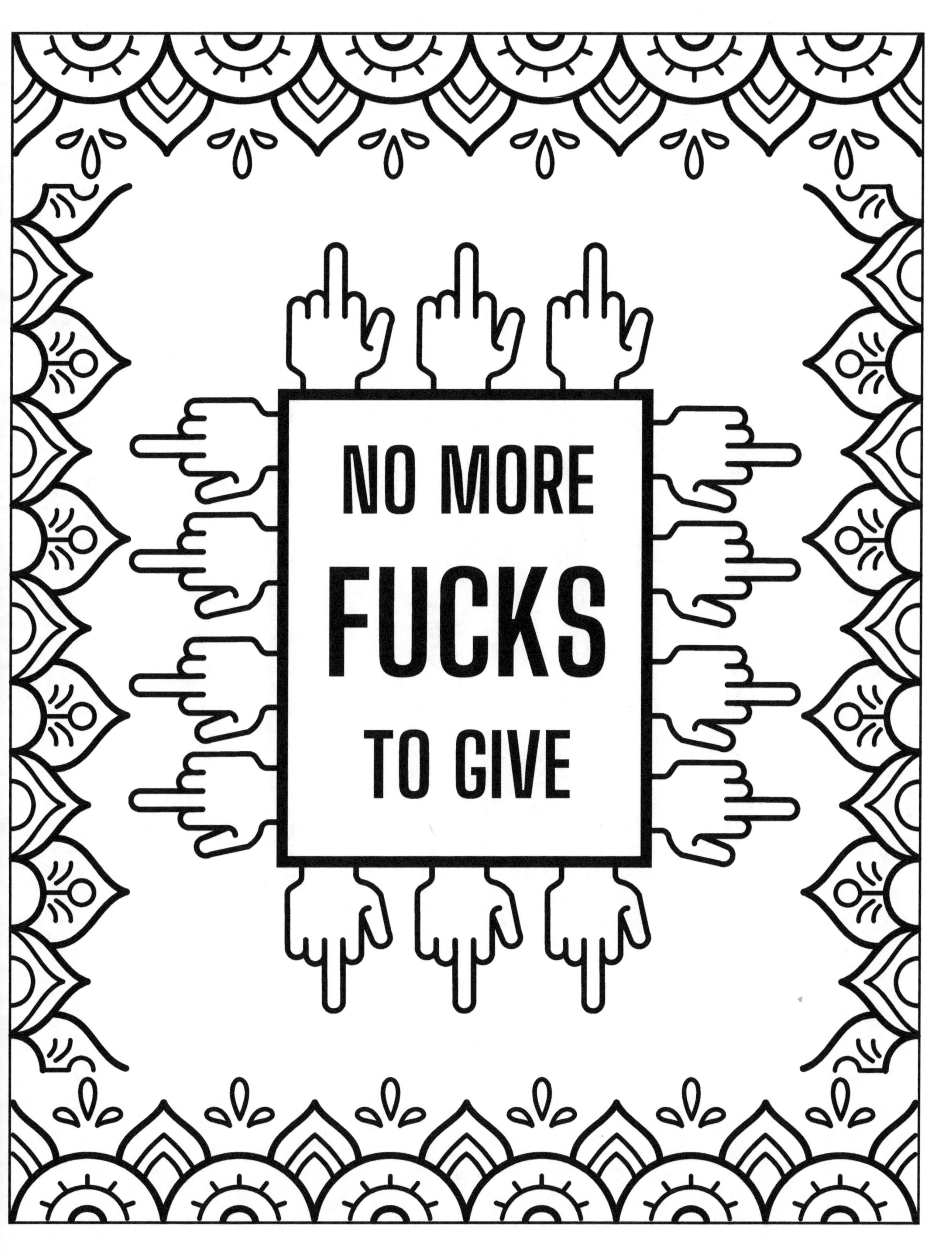
NO MORE
FUCKS
TO GIVE

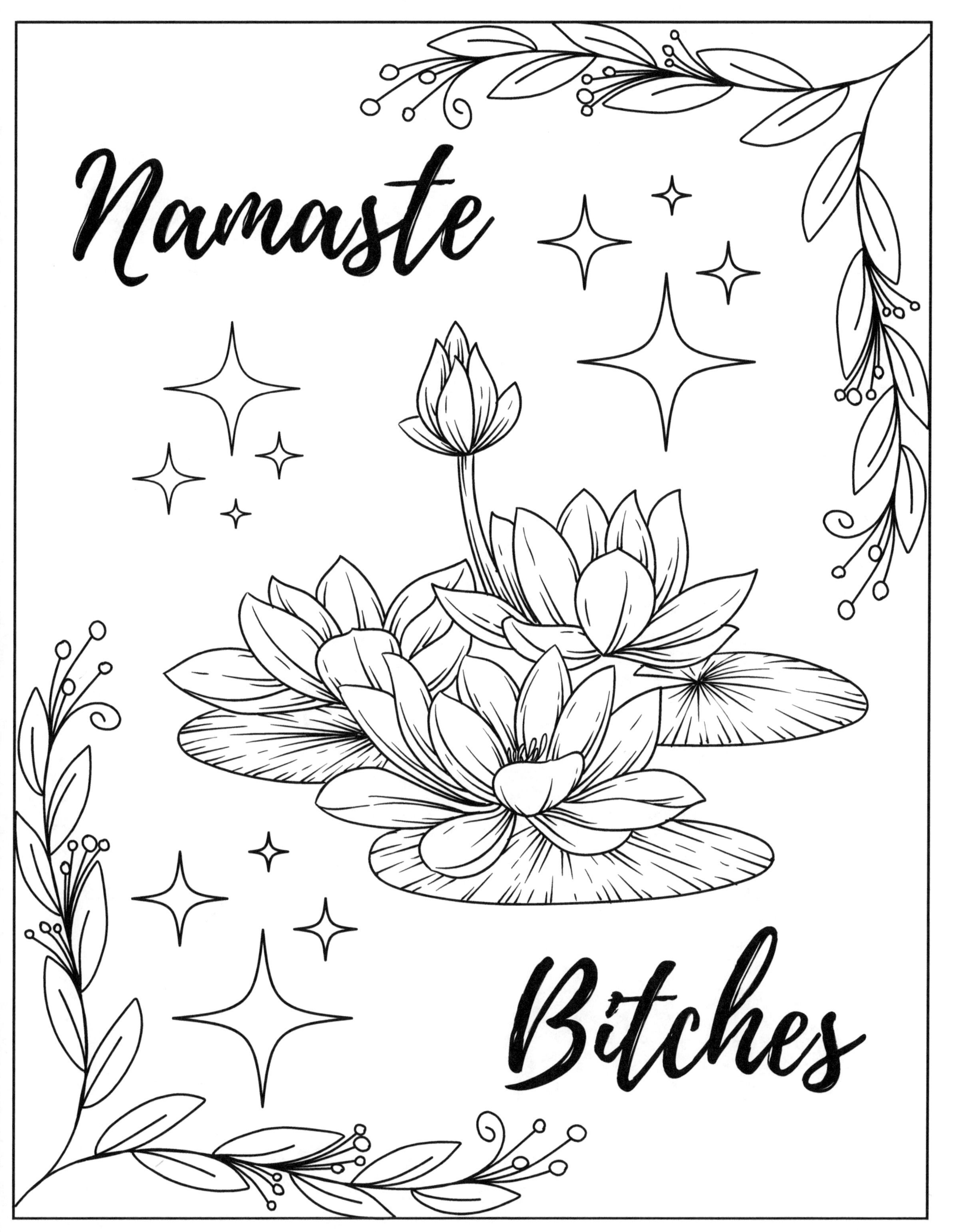
Namaste
Bitches

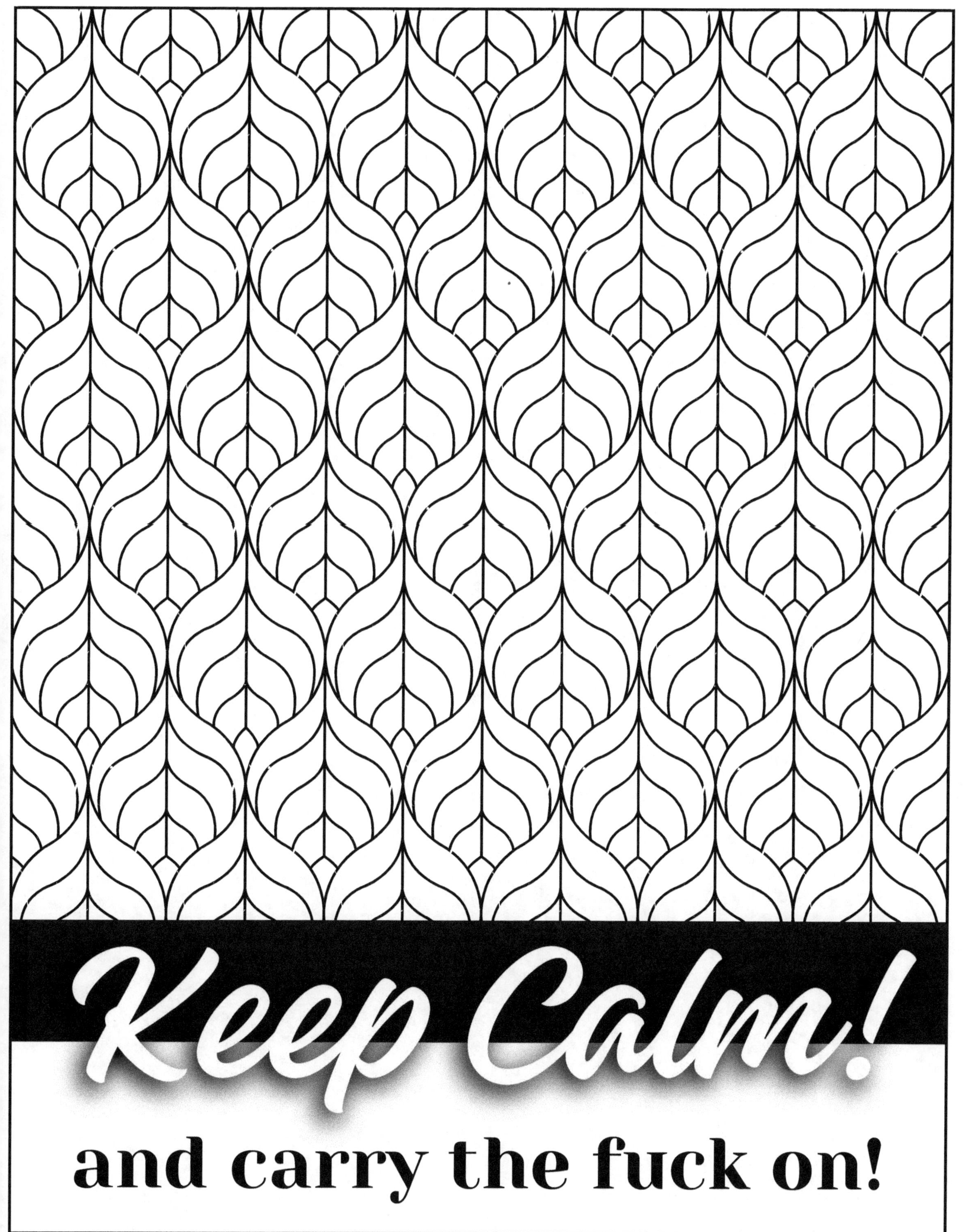
Keep Calm!
and carry the fuck on!

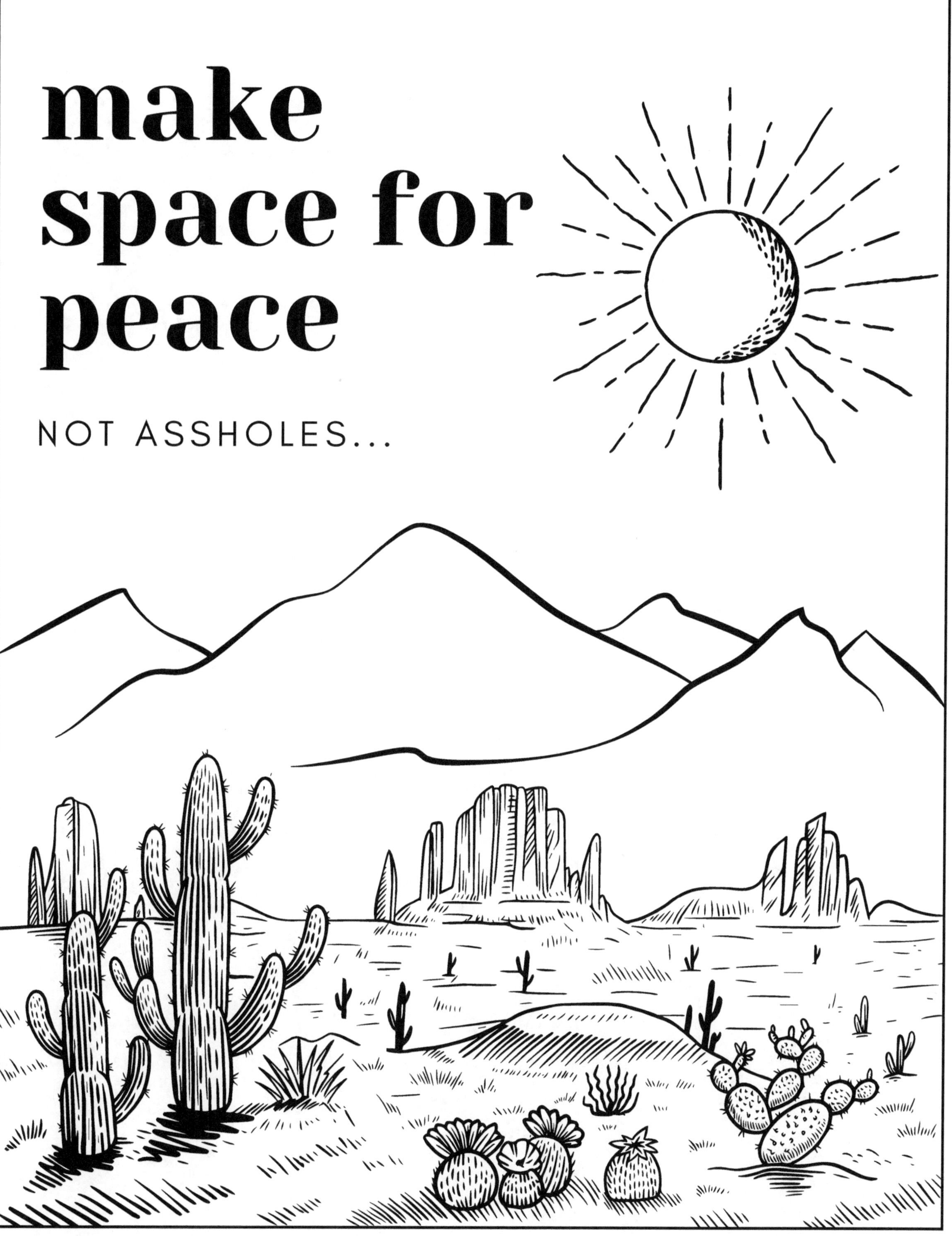
make
space for
peace
NOT ASSHOLES...

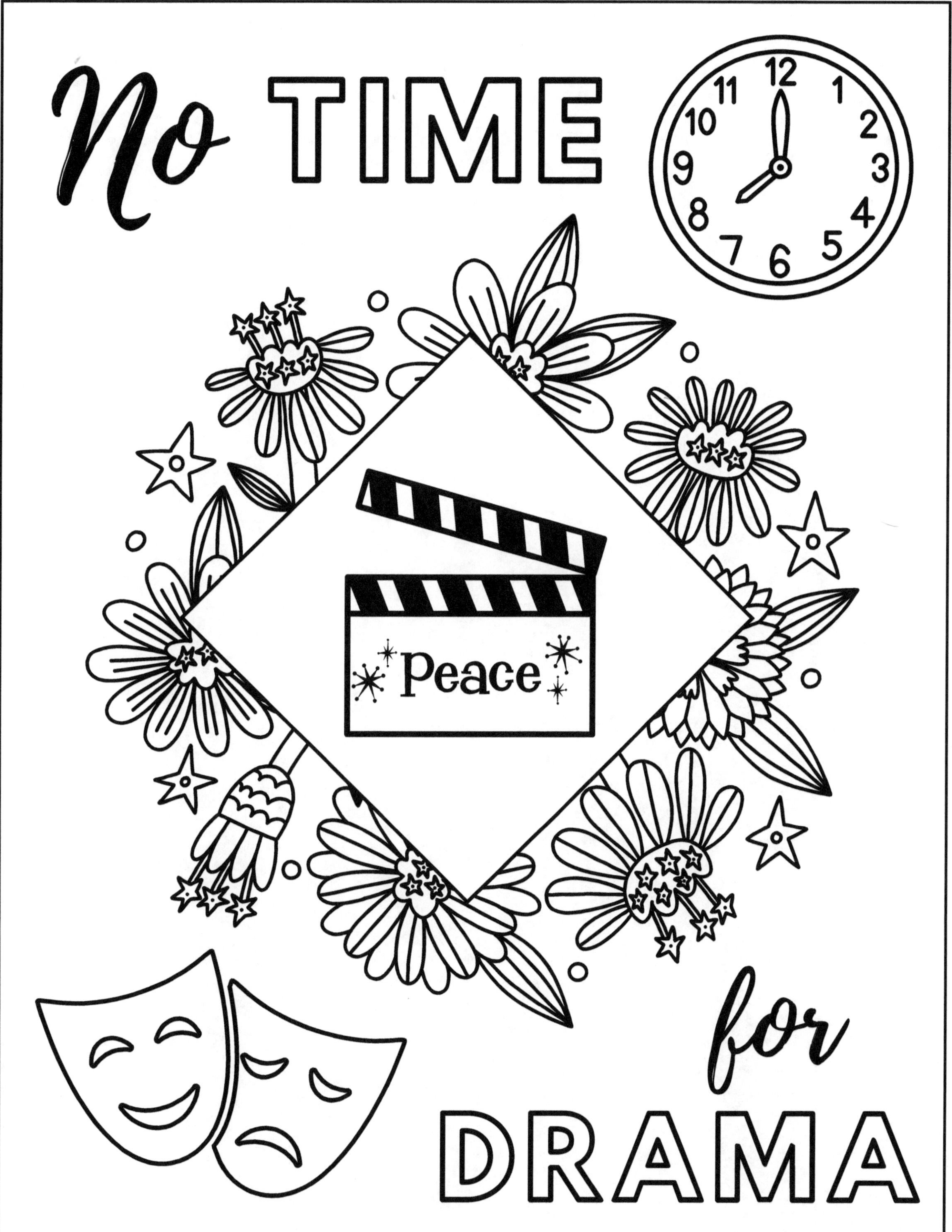
No TIME
12
1
2
3
4
5
6
7
8
9
10
11
Peace
for
DRAMA

MEDITATE

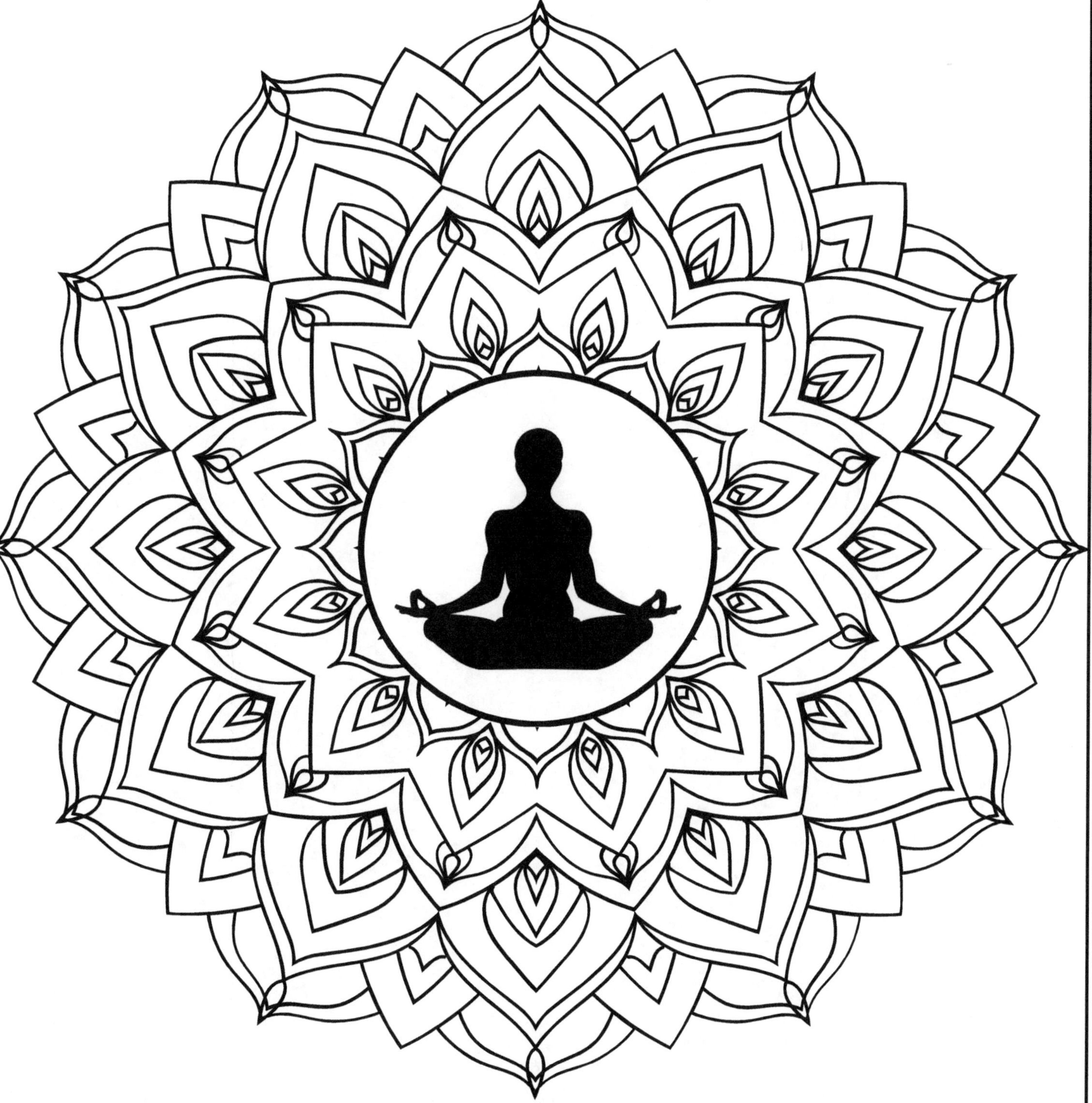

BECAUSE PRISON SUCKS!

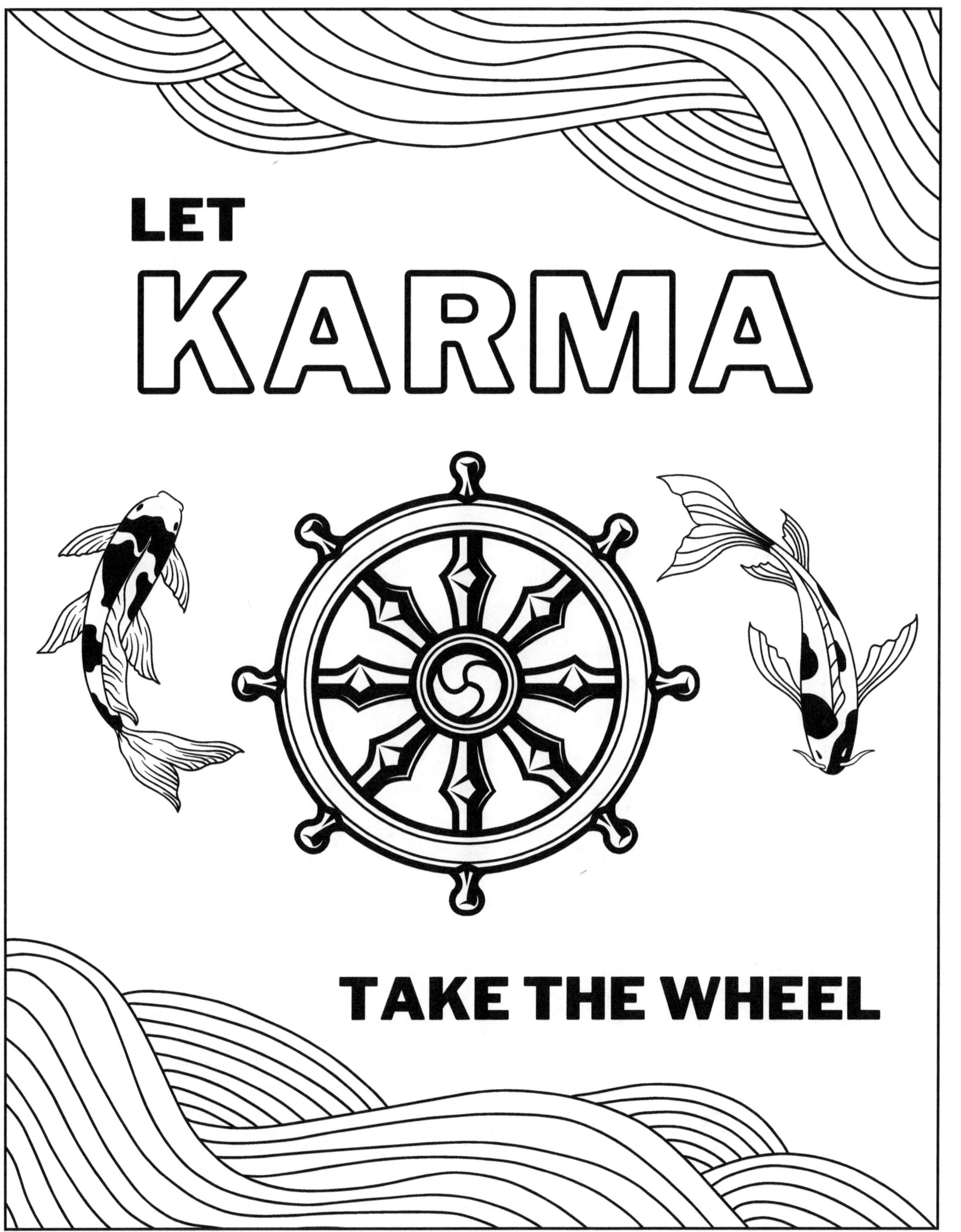
LET
KARMA
TAKE THE WHEEL

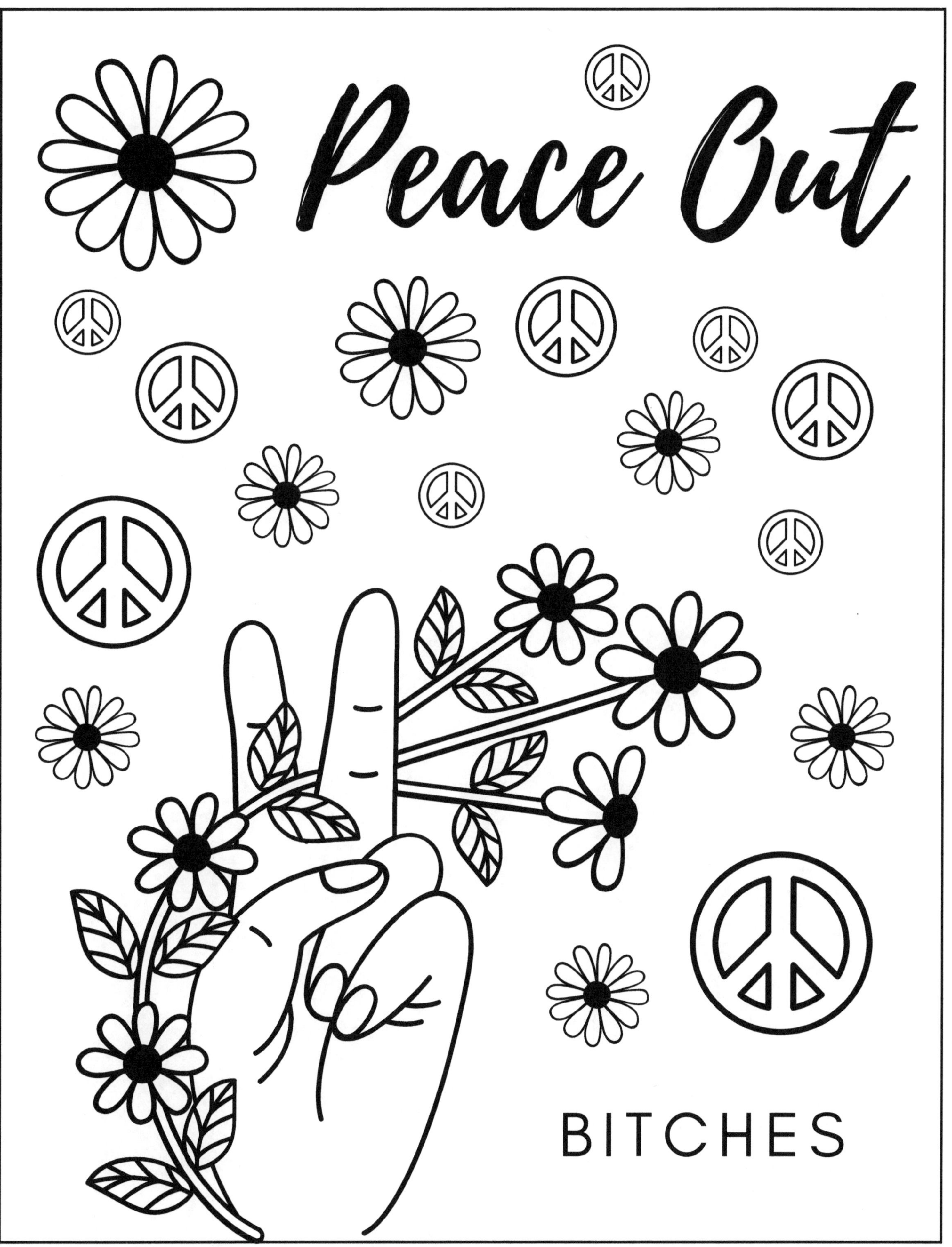
Peace Out
BITCHES

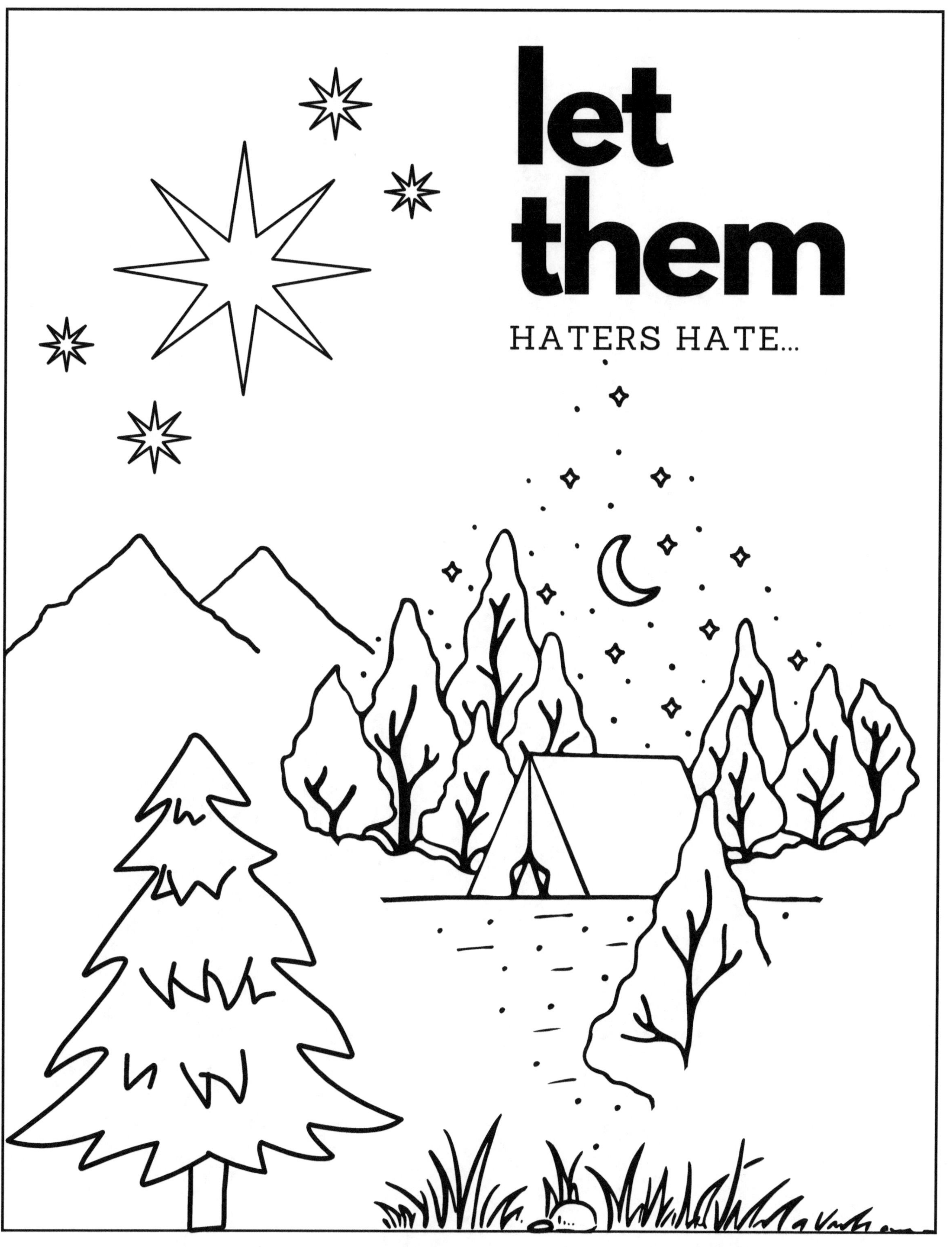
let
them
HATERS HATE...

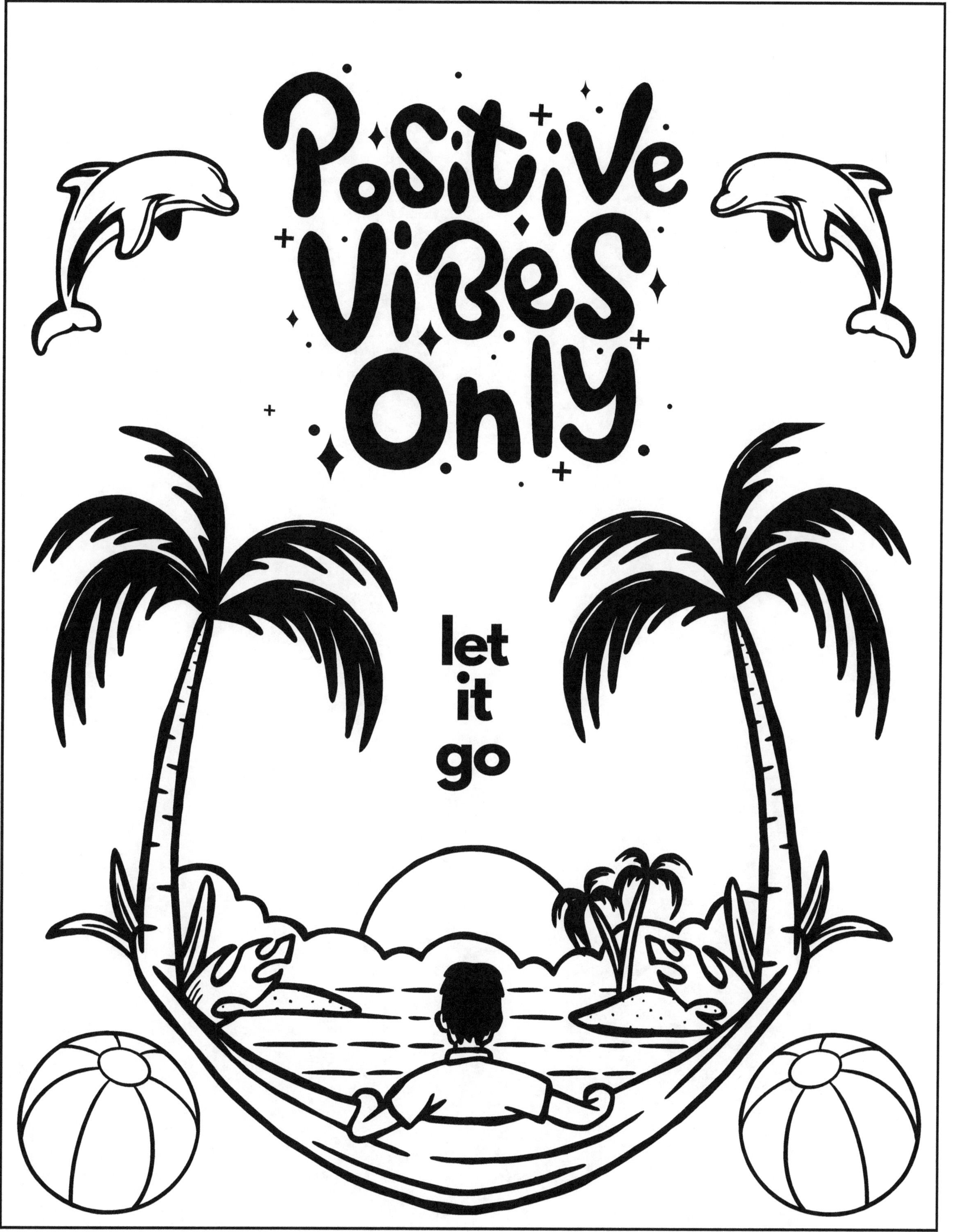
Positive
Vibes
Only
let
it
go

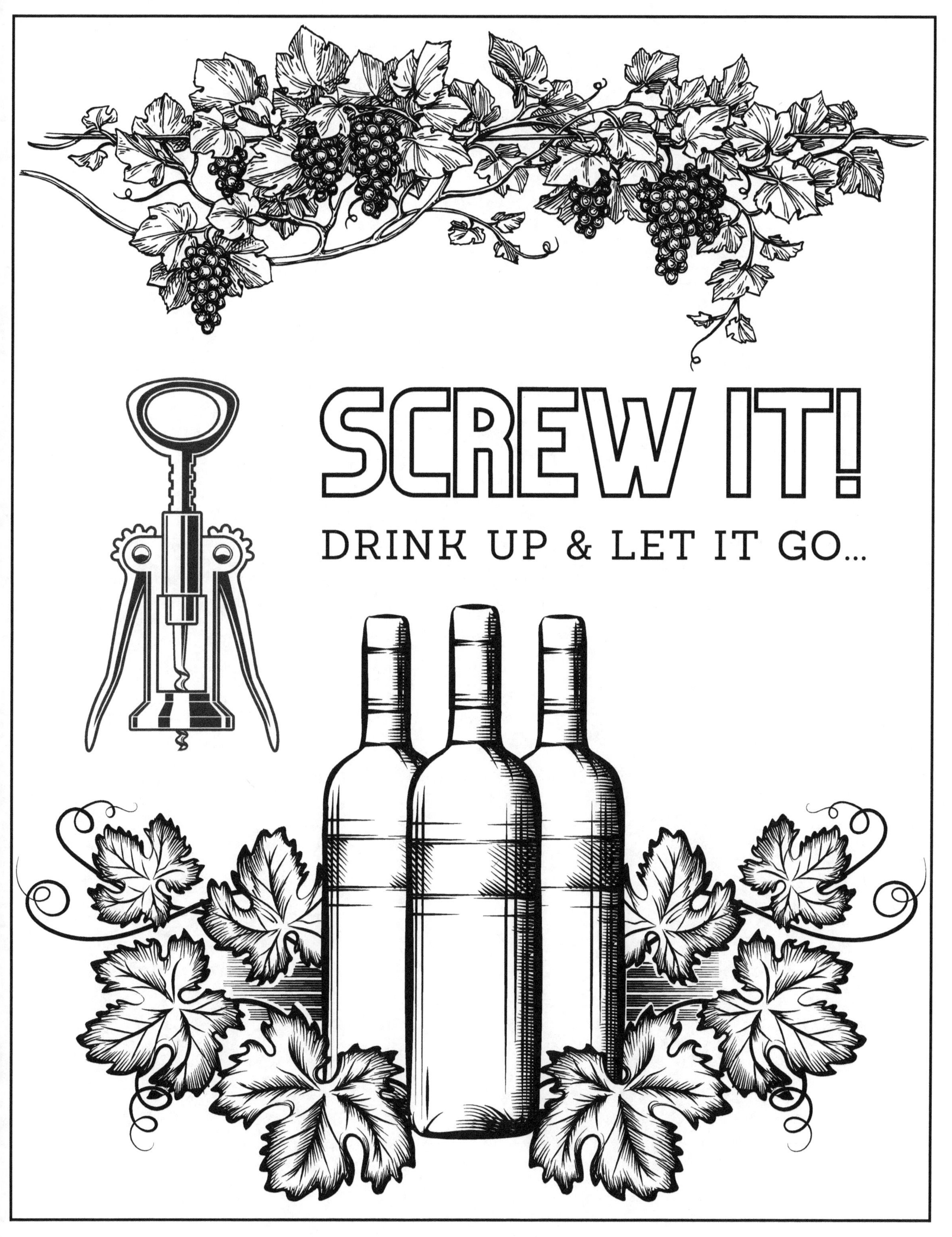
SCREW IT!
DRINK UP & LET IT GO...

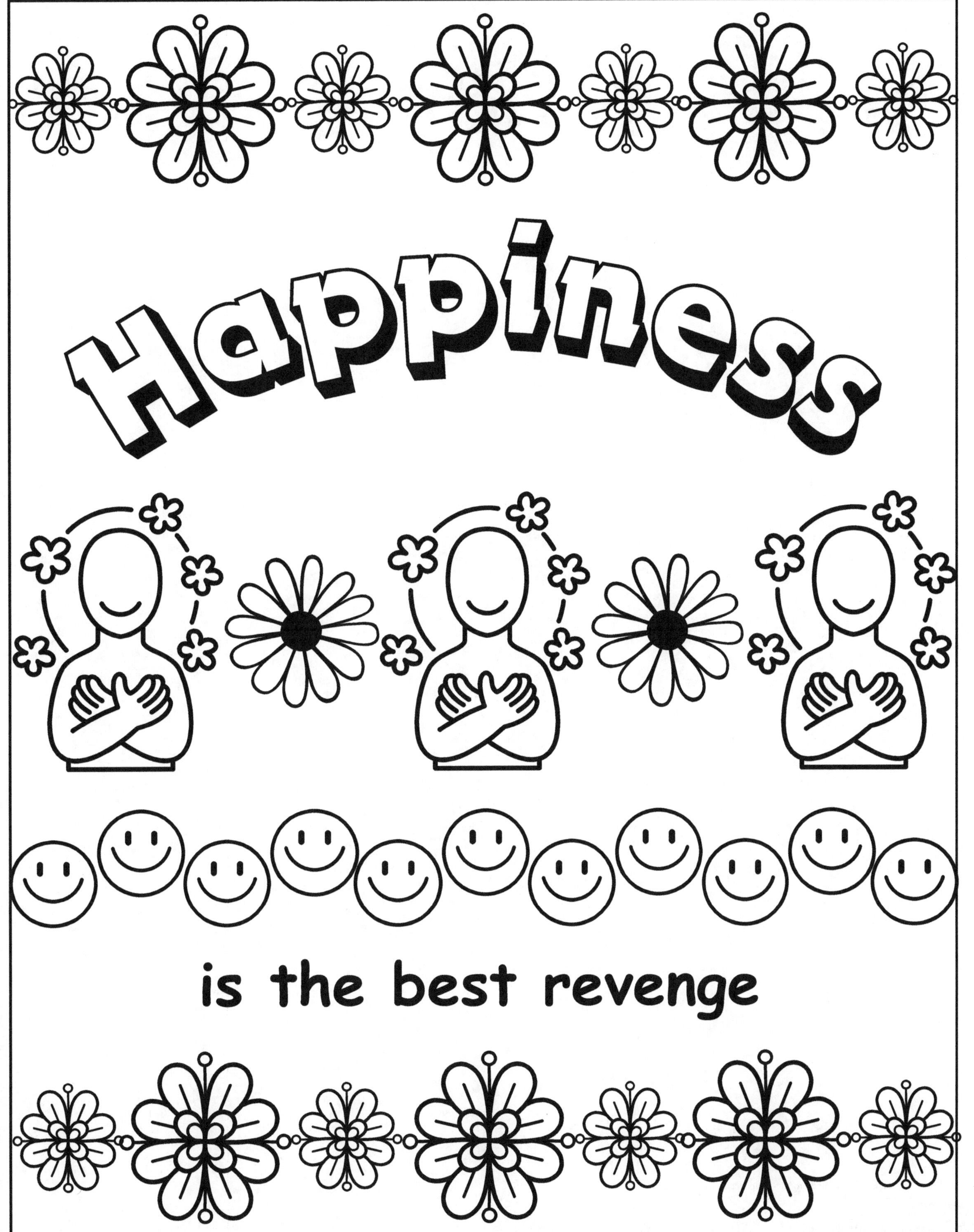
Happiness
is the best revenge

www.ingramcontent.com/pod-product-compliance
Lightning Source LLC
LaVergne TN
LVHW081425110826
845149LV00010B/1869

* 9 7 9 8 9 8 9 8 4 5 7 0 5 *